Fun with Math

by Bryan H. Bunch

Published by

World Book Encyclopedia, Inc.
a Scott Fetzer company

Chicago

Printed in the United States of America
ISBN 0-7166-3159-8
Library of Congress Catalog Card No. 82-51274
b/hd

Introduction

Have you ever wondered how you can win every time at games like Tic Tac Toe or Supergeography? Have you ever wished you could always find logic where you needed it? Have you ever wanted to find solutions to number puzzles easily, without worrying that math is involved?

If your answer to any of these questions is yes, then you need to sit down and start reading and working through *Fun with Math*. This delightful new publication from World Book contains many pages of fun, including mathematical puzzles, games, and logic problems. It also shows many strategies for participating and winning these games.

You will need to put on your thinking cap and use your powers of reasoning and observation to solve the many interesting and enjoyable mathematical diversions that are included. There are games and puzzles that can be played with paper and pencils, coins, toothpicks, or markers, along with some games and puzzles that require none of these materials. Some of the puzzles involve more advanced mathematical theory—however, all can be solved by common sense or trial-and-error experimentation.

Simply by solving these problems and puzzles, you may find that you know more math than you thought. But if a puzzle seems difficult, do not give up. Try drawing a diagram or writing down known information before looking at the answer.

In this book, you will discover some of the most exciting puzzles, games, and other mathematical materials available. *Fun with Math* has many hours of challenge and pleasure waiting for you.

Contents

Fun with Puzzles

Puzzle Number

Fun with Games

Fun with Numbers

Fun with Geometry

Fun with Paradoxes

Answers

Fun with Puzzles

1. The Coin in the Glass

Many puzzles can be made from coins or toothpicks. Here is one that uses both a coin and toothpicks.

Four toothpicks are used to form a glass with a stem. A coin is in the glass. You must get the coin out of the glass by moving two, and only two, toothpicks. You may not move the coin. There is, of course, a catch. After you have moved the toothpicks, you must have also re-formed a glass with a stem.

Hint: The following requires moving only two toothpicks, but it is not a solution. Although it is all right for the glass to be upside down, the coin is still inside the glass.

2. Just Toothpicks

Use eighteen toothpicks to form six squares as shown in the diagram below.

You are to remove two of the toothpicks so that the remaining figure forms exactly four squares. You cannot have a toothpick left that is not a side of one of the squares. How can you do it?

3. Just Coins

Use ten coins that are all alike, pennies, for example. Make them into a triangle that has four coins in the bottom row, three coins in the next, two coins in the next, and a single coin at the top.

Now form another triangle just like the one shown, but upside down. You are allowed to move only three coins, however.

Hint: It may help to start with a simpler problem. Make a triangle of six coins, three in the bottom row, two in the next, and one on top. Now turn the triangle upside down in two moves.

4. The Spy and the Drums

Coin and toothpick puzzles may not seem very practical. In special cases, however, the solution to a coin puzzle can be used somewhere else.

You are a spy trapped in a warehouse. There is no obvious place to hide, but there are six tall drums arranged as shown.

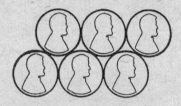

You have just enough time to move two of these drums to form a closed circle, with you safe in the middle. However, when you move the first drum, you discover that it must be touching two other drums to stay upright. How can you move just two drums so that at the end of each move all drums touch two other drums and after two moves form the circle? This is a lot like the coin puzzle of turning the triangle upside down. If you represent the drums with coins, you can solve the puzzle by moving the coins. The solution requires that you move the coins from the parallelogram shape shown above so that they form a circle as shown on page 11. Only one coin may be moved at a time, at the end of each move it must be touching two other coins, and only two moves are permitted.

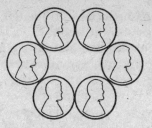

5. The Spy and the Lock

Here is a more fanciful situation that can also be solved as a coin problem. You are once again a spy, having escaped by solving the problem of the drums. Now you have to break into a wall safe that contains important enemy secrets. You have learned that the safe has an unusual lock. There is a row of eight buttons on the front of the safe. Each button can be pulled out of the safe a short distance and slid along to where it can be placed on top of another button. The safe will open when all of the buttons have been paired in this way, provided the pairing is correct. You have been able to learn that each button must pass over exactly two buttons in each move (and that there is only one solution). That is, a button being moved can pass over two individual buttons or over exactly one pair of buttons. It has something to do with magnets. You also learn that only the one move is to the left; all other moves go to the right.

For convenience, the buttons are numbered as shown.

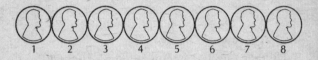

Incidentally, you must get it right the first time—that is, in only four moves—or the safe will explode.

Turn this into a coin problem by using coins for the buttons. Place eight coins in a row. Then move four coins so that each one passes over exactly two of the other coins. If you do it right, the result will be four stacks of two coins each.

6. A More Difficult Problem Emerges
You work out the solution to the problem of the safe at home with a group of eight coins. However, when you sneak into the enemies' hideout and find the safe behind the picture, you find that you have been slightly misinformed (or else the lock has been changed). Instead of eight buttons, there are ten in a row.

You correctly deduce that the same rules apply, but this time you must get five buttons paired in five moves. As before, each button must pass over exactly two buttons, either separate or paired, for the safe to open. You also correctly assume only one move goes to the left. How do you solve this one?

7. Planning Gardens

Four families decide to buy a vacant lot in their neighborhood so that they have room for vegetable gardens. The lot is L-shaped. Each family is to have its own garden.

To be fair, the families agree that each one should have a garden area that is the same shape and the same area. How can you separate the lot into four garden plots that match these requirements?

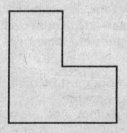

The two longest sides of the lot are exactly twice as long as the four shorter sides, which are equal in length. The angles are all right angles. Copy the drawing on a sheet of paper (scale does not matter). You need to show the borders that divide this lot into four congruent (same size and shape) sections.

8. Connect the Dots

There are a lot of puzzles that involve diagrams drawn on paper. Draw a set of nine dots on a sheet of paper to form a square as shown.

Now draw four line segments—parts of straight lines—that connect all nine dots. As usual, there are some rules you have to follow:

1. Each dot must be on at least one line segment.
2. You cannot pick up your pencil. In other words, each new line segment must begin at the end of the line segment you have just drawn.

3. You cannot retrace any of the line segments, but it is all right for one segment to cross another one.

You may think that this cannot be done after you have tried it a few times. It can be done, however. Just make sure that you do not mentally add a fourth rule to the ones given.

9. Connecting More Dots

If you can solve the problem with nine dots, you can probably solve it with sixteen. The solution is not exactly the same, however, so it may take a few tries to get it right. Follow the same three rules as for nine dots, but this time you are allowed to use six line segments to connect the dots.

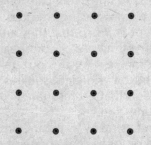

10. Planting a Grove

Here is a "practical" problem that can be solved as a coin problem but that also has some elements in common with connecting the dots.

A farmer wants to plant a grove of nine trees. The farmer is extremely orderly. All the trees are to be in rows of three. This does not sound very difficult, but the farmer has made it more difficult than it sounds. There must be ten straight rows, each with three trees in a row. (A square pattern of dots like the one shown in puzzle 8 will have eight straight rows of three trees; three horizontal, three vertical, and two diagonal.)

A good way to solve this problem is with nine coins. If you can arrange the nine coins in ten rows of three, you have the solution.

11. A Checkerboard Problem

In the last puzzle, it was necessary to put trees (or coins) in line. Now consider the opposite problem—placing checkers, chess pieces, or coins so that they are not in line. If you have a checkerboard handy, you can use it for this puzzle. Otherwise, draw a grid eight squares by eight squares so that each square is big enough for one coin.

You can put as many as eight coins on such a board or grid so that none of them is in line, either horizontally, vertically, or along any one of the diagonals. If you play chess, then think of the coins as queens. The object is to put eight queens on the board so that none of them can attack any one of the others. (This is not a different problem; just another way to think of the same problem.)

12. The Nonattacking Chess Pieces

The last puzzle could be stated as a chess problem: How many queens could you put on a chessboard so that none of them could attack another one? It is interesting to try the same problem with other chess pieces. Try the following variation: How many rooks can you put on a chessboard so that none of them can attack another one? If you do not know chess, then you need to know that a rook can only move along a row or column.

13. Keeping the Knights Out of Trouble

A much more interesting problem is the following: How many knights can you put on the chessboard so that none can attack another one?

A knight moves in a very odd way. For each move, the knight goes two squares in one direction along a row or column and one square at a right angle to the first direction. The knight can only attack the last square on which it lands. Therefore, for each knight, there are eight squares it can attack. These are shown on a section of a chessboard on page 18.

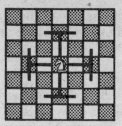

Despite the complexity of the knight's possible moves, the solution to this puzzle is actually quite easy—once you have the right idea.

If you do not play chess, however, you might need a hint. You should read the following hint only if you are not a chess player or if you have already tried to solve the problem and failed.

Hint: Notice that the knight always attacks a square different from the color of the one it is on when it starts the move.

14. Getting to the Island

A square backyard swimming pool has a square island in the middle of it. The pool is ten meters by ten meters, and the island is two meters by two meters. You want to sunbathe on the island, but you cannot swim and there is no raft. However, there are two fairly wide boards lying beside the pool. You could walk out to the island on one of those except that when you try, you discover that each one is just a few centimeters short of reaching the island.

How can you use the two boards to reach the island? There are no nails or rope handy, so there is no way to nail or tie the boards together. Although the boards float, even taken together they are not able to hold you out of the water when used as a raft.

A good way to treat this problem is to make a toothpick-and-drawing model of it. Use one toothpick as a unit four meters long. Then the drawing should be made with the pool 2½ toothpicks square and the island ½ toothpick square. You should be able to use two toothpicks on the drawing to show a way to get to the island.

15. The Farmer, the Baker, and the Cook
While standing in line at the supermarket one day, Mrs. Cook realized that her friends Mr. Farmer and Miss Baker were right behind her in line. When she discovered that they did not know each other, she introduced them, saying, "Isn't this odd. Here we are, a farmer, a baker, and a cook. But none of us has the name that goes with our job."

The baker replied, "That really is odd."
Which name goes with which job?

16. Another Supermarket Puzzle

In that same supermarket, three students worked as stock helpers. Stock helpers either stock shelves with groceries or help bag groceries. The three stock helpers' names are Don, Terry, and Cynthia.

Every day the supermarket manager assigns the stock helpers to their jobs for the day. The manager follows these rules:

1. Either Don or Cynthia will stock shelves, but not both.
2. If Don stocks shelves, then Terry will bag groceries.
3. Terry and Cynthia will not both bag groceries.

Using these three rules, which one of the stock helpers could have both stocked shelves yesterday and bagged groceries today?

17. Lewis Carroll's Logic

Lewis Carroll, who wrote *Alice in Wonderland*, was really the mathematician Charles Lutwidge Dodgson. He often combined his interest in logic with his wild imagination to invent puzzles similar to "The Farmer, the Baker, and the Cook." In Carroll's puzzles, he presented a series of statements that he claimed to be true. The object is to use all of the statements together to produce a single conclusion.

Here is one of his problems. The five true statements are:

1. All writers who understand human nature are clever.
2. No one is a true poet unless he can stir the hearts of men.
3. Shakespeare wrote *Hamlet*.
4. No writer who does not understand human nature can stir the hearts of men.
5. No one but a true poet could have written *Hamlet*.

What conclusion can you reach?

18. More of Lewis Carroll's Logic
If you enjoyed figuring out Lewis Carroll's reasoning in **17,** then try this one, which is more difficult. Remember that you must accept all the statements as true, even if you do not agree with them.

1. The only animals in this house are cats.
2. Every animal that loves to gaze at the moon is suitable as a pet.
3. When I hate an animal, I avoid it.
4. No animals are carnivores unless they prowl at night.
5. No cat fails to kill mice.

6. No animals ever take to me but the ones in this house.
7. Kangaroos are not suitable as pets.
8. Only carnivores kill mice.
9. I hate animals that do not take to me.
10. Animals that prowl at night always love to gaze at the moon.

You must use all ten statements to reach the correct conclusion.

19. Three Bags Full

Once again you are a spy. Your job is to steal a bag of top-secret documents from a messenger on a plane. You know that he is carrying three bags of messages. One bag contains nothing but documents marked "top secret." Another contains nothing but unmarked documents that are of no interest, since they are ordinary letters. The third bag contains some ordinary letters and some documents marked "top secret."

You can steal exactly one bag and place it in a secret compartment in your briefcase. Naturally, you want the bag that contains nothing but top secrets. The three bags are all labeled. One is labeled "secrets," one is labeled "letters," and the last is labeled "letters and secrets." However, to confuse possible spies, the messenger has deliberately labeled every bag with the wrong label.

While the messenger is distracted by the flight attendant, you have the chance to slip one document out of one bag and look at it. Since you learn whether that document is stamped "top secret" or not, you also know which bag to steal.

How do you do it? In other words, how can you look at one document from one of the bags and determine which bag really contains all top secrets?

20. A Weighty Puzzle
A druggist uses a balance scale and some weights to weigh the ingredients in prescriptions. Although the druggist has only four weights, she can weigh any amount from one gram to forty grams. What sizes are the four weights?

Be sure you know how a balance scale works. You put the object to be weighed on one side of the scale and one or more of the weights on the other. If the scale balances, the object weighs exactly the same as the weight(s), whose weight is known.

If the procedure described above were the only one you could use, however, you would need more than four different weights to weigh all amounts between one gram and forty grams. There is another procedure that also works. Suppose you have a five-gram weight and a two-gram weight, but you need three grams of a particular ingredient. Then you can put the five-gram weight on one side of the balance scale and the two-gram weight on the other. Then, you add the ingredient to the two-gram side until the scale balances. You will have three grams of the ingredient.

The pharmacist uses both procedures. Sometimes there are two, three, or even four weights on a single side of the balance.

Again, the puzzle is to determine the sizes of the four weights that can weigh all whole-number amounts from one gram to forty grams.

21. The Spy and the Coins

It is rumored that a version of this puzzle was planted by enemy agents during World War II. The puzzle was floated among the scientists working on the war effort in Britain. The scientists wasted so much time trying to solve it, the war effort was considerably slowed down. The version of the puzzle presented here is much easier, however.

Among a dozen identical coins, it is known that one is a fake. The fake coin can be recognized because it is slightly heavier than a true coin. The difference is too slight to be detected simply by holding the coins in your hand.

You are a captured spy, due to be executed in three days. Each day you are interrogated for one hour by an enemy officer, who has the coins lying on his desk along with a balance scale, but no set of weights. The fake coin is actually the missing piece of a secret radio transmitter, the other pieces of which are in your prison cell. You could safely remove the fake coin from the pile of coins without it being noticed, but you are sure to be caught if you take the whole pile. There is a brief moment during each interrogation when the officer leaves you alone. You have just enough time to use the balance scale to weigh the coins once. Fortunately, each of the twelve coins has a different date, so you can memorize the results of each weighing. If you can detect and steal the fake coin by the third day, you can complete the radio and call for help. Otherwise you will be executed.

To solve this problem, then, you must find the fake coin by determining which coin weighs more than the others within three weighings. You will not have time for a fourth weighing.

Hint: You need to weigh the coins in groups.

Fun with Games

22. Toe Tac Tic

Tit, tat, toe,
My first go,
Three jolly butcher boys all in a row.
Stick one up, stick one down,
Stick one in the old man's crown.

The nursery rhyme celebrates Tic Tac Toe, a game almost everyone knows how to play. Two sets of parallel lines are drawn to make nine squares. The first player puts an X in one of the squares. The second player puts an O in a different square. This continues until one player either has three X's in a row or three O's in a row or until all nine squares are filled. If a player gets three in a row, he or she is the winner. Otherwise the game is a tie (draw).

The first game for which children learn a good strategy is Tic Tac Toe, although the strategy is *not* the one in the old nursery rhyme. You cannot always win at Tic Tac Toe, but you can always draw if you put an X in the middle square and play carefully thereafter. Although putting an X in the middle square guarantees a draw, it is a poor way to win against an inexperienced player. Putting an X in one of the corners is much safer, since the inexperienced player has only one safe move, an O in the center. If she or he does not make that move, you have the game sewn up. Try it.

Variations on Tic Tac Toe are more interesting. Another way to play the game is as Toe Tac Tic. The first player to get three counters in a row loses. Otherwise the rules are the same. The game is no harder to play than Tic Tac Toe, but the change in rules makes it quite different when you first start playing.

Although it seems unlikely, unless the first player makes exactly the right move, the second player can always win or draw at Toe Tac Tic. Try playing a few games. Can you figure out the correct strategy for the first player to follow to always insure at least a draw?

23. Movable Tic Tac Toe

The Romans played Tic Tac Toe with counters that could be moved. Each player got only three counters. You can play the game using small pieces of cardboard marked with X's and O's as counters. The object of the game is the same as in ordinary Tic Tac Toe—to get three of your counters in a row, either across, up-down, or diagonally. If one player does not succeed when all six counters are placed on the board the first time—which is not likely—the players take turns moving the counters. The rule, however, is that a counter can only be moved a single square to the left or right or a single square up or down. You cannot move diagonally, and you cannot jump another counter as you can in checkers. While thoughtful play by both players will always lead to a draw, movable Tic Tac Toe is much trickier than ordinary Tic Tac Toe.

24. Tac Tix

A reverse version of the game with movable counters was invented by the Danish mathematician and poet, Piet Hein. It is called Tac Tix. It begins with all the counters already in place, and the players remove them. Since either player can remove any counter, the counters are not marked with X's and O's.

More than a single counter at a time can be taken from the board. The rule, however, is that only counters that are next to each other in the same row or the same column can be taken in a single move. For example, you might take either one, two, or all three counters from the top row, but you could not take just the two end counters (*see* illustration p. 30).

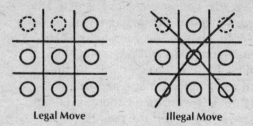

Legal Move   **Illegal Move**

The player who takes the last counter loses. Try playing a few games.

There are several winning strategies for the first player when played on a three-by-three board. Can you find them?

Tac Tix becomes much more interesting when played as *Extended Tac Tix* on a larger board with more counters. A four-by-four board using sixteen counters provides a number of interesting problems. The rules are almost the same as in three-by-three Tac Tix. Sixteen counters are arranged in four rows of four. You can remove any number of counters that are next to each other in a row or a column in a single move. The players alternate moves. The player who takes the last counter loses.

A detailed analysis shows that the second player can always win, but there is no single strategy that guarantees a win. (On boards with an odd number of counters in each side of the square, it is fairly easy for the first player always to win.) If you get tired of the four-by-four board, however, the six-by-six board with thirty-six counters makes for an interesting game.

25. The Game of HOT

Make nine cards from cardboard (or paper). On each card, print one of the following words, so that each card has a different word on it.

HOT	HEAR	TIED
FORM	WASP	BRIM
TANK	SHIP	WOES

To play the game, all the cards are placed face up in front of two players. The players alternate in taking cards. The first player to get three cards that have the same letter on them is the winner. Play a few games of HOT with a friend. It is not very difficult, but it is tricky.

Here is a problem you can solve about HOT. If both players always make the best move, will the first player always win, will the second player always win, or will the game end in a draw?

Hint: Draw a large Tic Tac Toe diagram on a sheet of paper. See if you can arrange the cards from HOT in the squares of the diagram so that each row, column, and diagonal contains a winning group of three cards.

26. How to Get from Girl to Boy

This is a game you can play with a pencil and paper and any number of other players. Choose a word, such as *girl*. Then choose another word, such as *boy*. The rules are that you are to change one word to another by changing one letter at a time. You can only replace a letter with another if the replacement makes a word, however. For example, if you are trying to get from *girl* to *boy*, you can replace the *r* with *l* to get *gill*, but you cannot replace the *r* with *y*, since that would make *giyl*, which is not a word in English. Also, you are allowed to assume that there is a blank letter at the beginning and end of each word. Therefore, you can add one letter at a time by replacing the blank with a single letter, either at the beginning or end of the word. You can shorten a word by replacing the letter at the end or the beginning with the blank. In playing the game, you can make the word shorter, then longer, then shorter as many times as you like.

Each change of a letter is counted as one move. The object of the game is to get from the first word chosen to the second word chosen in the fewest number of moves. A round of the game is over when one of the players believes that he or she has found the fewest number of moves. If you are playing with several people, give each of the players who tie one point and a player who wins two points. The winner for each round gets to choose the two words for the next round. If there is a tie during a round, the person with the lowest total score gets to choose the next words. If the scores are tied, the person with the least number of points gets to choose. If there is a tie for this, draw straws. The first person with ten points wins.

Here is a sample game. The challenge is to get from *day* to *later*. One player wrote the following as the result in five moves.

DAY
RAY
RAT
RATE
LATE
LATER

I can get from *girl* to *boy* in seven moves. Can you do better?

27. Word Games for Long Car Trips

A great word game called Superghosts can be played by any number of players. The first player chooses a letter. The second player then puts another letter either in front of or behind the first letter. (In ordinary Ghosts, the letter must always be added at the end.) Each player, in turn, adds a letter either to the front or back. The first player to add a letter that spells a word (longer than three letters) gets a "ghost." Three ghosts and a player is out. The player remaining at the end is the winner.

The catch is that each player must try to spell some particular word. If a player is challenged, the player must be able to tell the word that is being spelled. Failing to do that, the player gets a "ghost." Otherwise, the challenger gets the "ghost." (If you plan to play this on a long trip, it is advisable to bring along a dictionary.)

Another word game for any number of players is Geography. In Geography, you play with names of states or countries instead of letters. Say you are playing with names of states. The first player names a state. The second player must name a state that has as the first letter of its name the last letter of the state previously named. When a player cannot think of a state that meets the rules, that player is out. The next player can either continue the chain or start with a new state not previously used. The last player to be in the game wins.

Just as Ghosts can be made into Superghosts, Geography can be made into Supergeography by allowing a player either to make a Geography move or to add to the other end of the chain. To add to the front of the chain, the last letter of the new state must be the first letter of the previous state in the chain.

While most such word games have no strategy, there are winning strategies at Geography and Supergeography because of the limited number of states and countries. Consider just Supergeography played with states. You can always win if there are just two players and you start first. How?

If there are exactly three players in Supergeography, how can the first player always win?

28. Hex

Piet Hein, who invented Tic Tax, also developed the game of Hex. Hex is played on a board that looks like part of a honeycomb. While the board can be any size, it is easier to learn the strategy of the game using a small board, such as four-by-four or five-by-five. The standard hex board, however, is eleven-by-eleven.

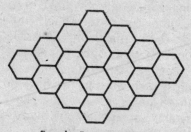

Four-by-Four Hex Board

Notice that each side of the board is labeled either X or O. (The game can also be played with counters. If so, and if the counters are black and white, then the sides of the board are labeled "black" and "white".) The corners of the board are considered to be both X and O at the same time. As in Tic Tac Toe, each player alternates in putting X's and O's into the hexagons on the board. Instead of trying to get a straight row, however, the object is to link your two sides of the board. That is, the first player, who uses X, wants to link the two sides of the board labeled X, while the second player wants to link the two sides of the board labeled O. At each turn, an X or an O can be put in any unoccupied hexagon.

The link between the two sides may twist and turn as much as it likes. Of course, it is possible for one player to block completely the other player's chain.

Unlike Tic Tac Toe, however, Hex can never end in a draw. Your first challenge is to explain why Hex cannot end in a draw.

On a four-by-four Hex board, one of the players can always win if he or she makes the first move. Play a few games on a four-by-four board. (If you have access to a copying machine, it helps to draw one board and then make a number of copies.) Which moves can a player make to always win?

Hint: There are four opening moves that guarantee one player will win. If that player does not make one of those moves, then the other player can win by making one of those moves. What are the four moves that will win the game?

On the standard eleven-by-eleven board, no one knows which opening moves would guarantee a win.

29. A Game of Cards

The following game has no strategy by which either player can guarantee a win. As a consequence, this is a good game that tests both players' skills. The game was invented by the mathematician Rufus Isaacs and named "Guess It" by his daughter Ellen. Here are the rules.

A deck of eleven cards is used, with the cards marked from 1 through 11. (If you use regular playing cards, the ace can be 1 and the jack can be 11.) After the cards have been shuffled, one card is dealt face down on the table. The two players are each dealt five cards.

Each player is to try to guess the number of the card that has been dealt face down. On each play, one player either asks the other if there is a particular card in the other's hand or else tries to name the card that has been dealt face down.

Suppose on the first play, the first player asks the second if the second has the 7. It is required that the players answer truthfully. Either the second player has the 7 or does not have it. If the second player has it, the card is put face up on the table. In that case it cannot be asked about again. If the second player does not have the card, then it is the second player's turn.

Now the second player may either guess the face-down card or ask the first player about some other card, say the 2. Or the second player may ask the first player if there is the 7 in the first player's hand. This is a difficult choice to make, since if the first player does *not* have the 7, the first player will know that the 7 is the face-down card. The first player can then name the face-down card and win. On the other hand, the first player may have been deliberately misleading the second player. That is, the first asked about the 7 even though the first player knew the second player did not have it.

This is a game that involves considerable psychology. Make a deck or use some playing cards and give it a try.

Fun with Numbers

30. Going Coco-nutty

There is a desert island on which the only trees are coconut palms. Although it is occasionally visited by birds, its sole mammal inhabitant is a single monkey, which has been stranded there for many years. The monkey lives on coconuts.

Since dangerous reefs are nearby, sailors often are shipwrecked on the island. Fortunately, they can live on the coconuts until they are rescued.

One year three sailors are shipwrecked on the island; a captain, a midshipman, and a common swab. The captain decides that the coconuts then available on the ground should be divided by rank. He takes half of the available coconuts, plus half a coconut. He allots half of the remaining coconuts to the midshipman, plus half a coconut. The swab also gets half the coconuts that are left plus half a coconut. There is still one coconut remaining, so it is tossed to the grateful monkey, since it is clear that more coconuts will be available the next day.

How many coconuts were available on the first day?

31. Counting 'em Out

Here is a puzzle that is easy to solve; although based on a practice that must be very old, it is as contemporary as the current generation of children: Counting Out. In the United States, the most common form of Counting Out is based on the following nursery rhyme:

> One potato, two potatoes,
>   three potatoes, four,
> Five potatoes, six potatoes,
>   seven potatoes, more . . .
> 1, 2, 3, YOU'RE OUT.

If you are a clever child, you can generally find the place to stand in the circle so that you will either be among the ones counted out or remaining at the end to be chosen. The first time around, the twelfth person counted will be out, since the counter points at a different person for each of the numbers. The second count begins with the one after the person counted out, and proceeds to continue counting around the circle, getting one more person out. This process can be repeated until only one lucky (or clever) child remains.

Suppose that there are seven children to be counted. If you wish to be the winner, at which position should you stand if the counter begins counting at position A? (*see* illustration, p. 42)

32. The Josephus Problem

An old Western story associated with counting concerns the time that a man named Josephus found himself with forty other people trapped in a cave by the enemy. At the back of the cave, there was a small, secret place where just two people could hide. The rest of the troop would undoubtedly be killed or captured, and, if captured, very likely tortured and then killed anyway. It was agreed that they would count out to determine which of the forty-one people would be safely hidden, while the rest would fight to the last.

It was decided to count every third person out, with the last two remaining to be the ones to hide. Josephus quickly determined where he and his best friend should stand. Assume that the count begins with a person numbered one. What are the numbers of the places where Josephus and his friend should stand to escape being counted out?

33. The Mathematical Heir

An Eastern version of a similar counting-out problem involves a man who had fifteen children when his first wife died. At that point, he remarried and had an additional fifteen children by his second wife. When he died, the second wife was still alive, but the man had left a will in which the estate was to go to one of his children. The man, however, had been unable to decide among the children as to who should be heir, so he directed that they be arranged in a circle and counted out by nines. Every ninth child would be eliminated, and the one remaining would inherit everything.

The widow was determined that the heir would be one of her own children, especially since all her stepchildren hated her. The night before the great counting out, she determined how to arrange the children so that when the first child was counted—by arrangement in the will, the youngest child had the honor of being counted first—all her stepchildren would be eliminated first and thereafter only her children would remain. She did not care which of her children was the heir, just so long as it was one of *hers*.

Call the children from the first marriage F's and the ones from the second marriage S's. How should the circle be arranged so that, if the count begins with an S and every ninth child is eliminated, all the F's will be eliminated in the first fifteen counts?

The story had a happy ending, however. One of the F's was a mathematician and soon perceived what was going to happen. The bright child took a place in the circle so that all the other F's would be eliminated first. Then, the last remaining F appealed to the stepmother, "All my brothers and sisters have been eliminated. The count is unfairly arranged. Please begin counting in the other direction so that I will have at least a small chance of inheriting." The stepmother, seeing fifteen S's and only a single F remaining, felt that it was quite safe to agree to the request. The count proceeded in the opposite direction. What was the result?

34. Mistaken Arithmetic

People often have trouble with fairly simple problems in mathematics. For example, what is the answer if you divide 50 by ½ and add 3? Don't be too sure that you have the right answer until you check with the answer section.

35. Finding the Errors
Detecting errors made by others or by yourself is not always easy. There are three errors for you to detect among the problems in this paragraph. Can you find all three?

A. $5\frac{2}{3} \times 2\frac{5}{6} = 16\frac{1}{18}$ B. $3.004 + 7.39 = 10.43$
C. $598 \div 24 = 24.916$ D. $3.09 \times 0.047 = 0.14523$
E. $\frac{4}{17} + \frac{7}{51} = \frac{1}{3}$

36. A Mathematical Fallacy
In mathematics, a fallacy is a result that seems plausible, but is actually wrong. Of course, any mistake honestly made in arithmetic seems plausible to the person making it at the time it is made, but the mistake becomes a fallacy when there is some reason given to explain the mistake.

For example, a student who has learned how to cancel in working with fractions may mistakenly apply the method where it does not work. You know that if you have a fraction such as

$$\frac{3 \times 4}{4 \times 5}$$

you can cancel to find the fraction in simplest form.

$$\frac{3 \times \cancel{4}}{\cancel{4} \times 5}$$

The result is $\frac{3}{5}$, which is correct. What happens when you apply the same method when the numerator and denominator are both sums instead of products? You probably know that in general you will get the wrong answer. Is there any set of three numbers a, b, and c, with a different from c and b not 0, so that the following procedure gives the correct results?

$$\frac{a + \cancel{b}}{\cancel{b} + c}$$

One student carried fondness for cancellation to the extreme of reducing the fraction $\frac{16}{64}$ by canceling the 6's. The result, of course, was correct, since $\frac{16}{64} = \frac{1\cancel{6}}{\cancel{6}4} = \frac{1}{4}$. Even though the result was correct, using this method was a fallacy, since the reasoning was wrong—and the proof of a fallacy is in the reasoning, not in the result. How is the student's solution to the problem different from the case of numerators and denominators that are sums?

There are, in fact, an infinite number of fractions that can be correctly canceled by the student's method, although they are not always easy to find. Can you find another example using just two-digit numbers in the numerator and the denominator? The idea is to be able to cancel the same digit in the numerator and denominator and produce the correct simplified form. Fractions in which the numerator and denominator are the same number do not count!

37. A College Prank

Fred's roommate was practicing his saxophone, so Fred borrowed his friend Bill's room as a place to work on his big term paper. He started at 12:45, but by 1:00 he knew he had made a false start, so he crumpled the sheet of paper, tossed it on the floor, and started over.

He started again. This time he wrote two pages in fifteen minutes, but it was another false start. At 1:15 Fred crumpled both sheets, tossed them on the floor, and started over. With the two false starts behind him, Fred was able to write four pages in the next quarter hour, but once again he was dissatisfied, crumpled the four sheets of paper and tossed them on the floor.

Then Fred sat and thought for fifteen minutes. At the end of fifteen minutes, although he had written nothing, he thought he ought to follow the pattern. So he took eight sheets of paper from his notebook, crumpled them, and threw them on the floor. After another fifteen minutes, he took sixteen sheets of paper, crumpled them, and threw them on the floor.

He suddenly realized that he could play a prank on Bill instead of writing the paper. He called his friends to help. Every fifteen minutes, Fred and his friends crumpled twice as many sheets of paper as they had the last time. Finally, at 4:00 Fred and his friends had completely filled Bill's room with crumpled sheets of paper.

If Fred had written two pages in the first fifteen minutes instead of one, and the same pattern of doubling the number of crumpled sheets each time had continued, how much sooner would the room have been filled? At what time would they have finished?

38. Ages and Birth Years

In general, if you know the year someone was born and the year it is now, you can (with some uncertainty caused by the date of birth) determine that person's age. Sometimes, however, people like to make you work to figure out their ages.

Mrs. Oleander, when asked by her grandson about her age, replied that in 1950 she was exactly $\frac{1}{29}$ as old as the year she was born. What year was that?

39. Another Age and Birth-Year Puzzle

Having figured out when Mrs. Oleander had been born, the grandson wanted to know when his grandfather had been born. His grandfather, however, was taking a nap, so the grandson again asked his grandmother.

Mrs. Oleander thought awhile and finally replied that there was one year when Mr. Oleander noticed that if his age were squared, the square was the year of his birth. What year was Mr. Oleander born?

40. Squaring the Ages Again

Mrs. Oleander added that Mr. Oleander had once noticed another odd fact about his age. At one time in his life, he noticed that if he squared the age of each of his nine children, the sum of the squares was equal to the square of his own age.

If his children were born at equal intervals (which they were), how old was Mr. Oleander when he noticed this odd coincidence? How old were each of the children at that time?

41. A Good Handshake All Around

Different cultures have different rules about handshakes. Americans, for example, shake hands more than Europeans do. But the Japanese, who never shook hands in their traditional culture (they bowed instead), have carried the American practice of shaking hands to new heights in business dealings in the United States.

As a result, at a conference between Japanese and American businesspeople in the United States, the conference often cannot begin until everyone in the room has shaken hands with every other person in the room.

Twenty-four persons are gathered for a conference of Japanese and American businesspeople in the United States. Everyone shakes hands with everyone else. If the conference begins at 9:00, each handshake takes thirty seconds, and twelve pairs of businesspeople are shaking hands simultaneously during each thirty-second period, at what time of day does the actual work of the conference begin?

42. Time and Work

Emily is sawing logs to use in her wood-burning stove. She starts work at 2:00 P.M., and by 2:12 she has sawed her first log into three smaller logs, but she thinks that they are too long for the stove.

She takes a large log that is identical to the first one, but this time she saws it into four smaller logs. Now she is pretty tired, so she takes a break.

At what time of day does Emily start her break?

43. More Time and Work

Elroy is setting type by hand for a book of poems which he has written. After setting the type for the poems, one poem to a page, he realizes that the pages should be numbered. Although it is already midnight, he wants to get the job finished, so he sets all the page numbers in their proper place. When he finally finishes the job, it is 3:30 A.M.

If it takes Elroy one minute to set a single digit properly on the page, how many poems has he written?

44. The Gym-Teacher's Problem

Mrs. Misako needed to order baseball gloves for her gym class. She planned to order one style for the boys and a different style for the girls. She knew that four of the girls were left-handed, so they would need left-handed gloves. She also knew that there were twenty-three boys in the class of fifty students, but she did not know how many of them were right-handed and how many were left-handed. One day, when all the students were in class, she asked everyone who was right-handed to raise his or her hand. Forty-four hands were raised.

How many right-handed and left-handed gloves of each style should she order?

45. More Problems for the Gym Teacher
One night Mrs. Misako faced another
problem. She had left her class records at
the school, but she needed to plan the
activities for the next few weeks. It was
spring, so everyone would either work
on softball or track. She could remember
that all twelve seventh-grade boys
wanted to play softball and fourteen
girls wanted track. She also could remember that there were twenty-two seventh graders and seventeen eighth-grade
girls. Also, all of the boys in eighth grade
wanted to try track. All of the rest of the
facts about the class escaped her, except
that the total number of students that
year was forty-eight.

Were there enough girls to form a
girl's softball team? (She would need at
least ten players and a manager.)

46. Short Takes
In the school senate, each member
of the senate is required to be on two of
the five standing committees. No two
committees can have more than one
member in common, but, in fact, each
pair of committees does have one member in common. How many school senators are there?

47. A weird animal lover decides that pets should have hats and shoes to be properly dressed. The animal lover orders thirty hats and fifty pairs of shoes for his pets. If he has only canaries and cats, how many of his pets are cats and how many are canaries?

48. Another pet lover, Maria, kept a pet frog. One day while Maria was changing the frog's water, the frog escaped, and Maria had to catch it. The frog had taken ten hops before Maria noticed it was gone. Maria then chased the frog, taking two steps every time the frog jumped three times. If each of Maria's steps is twice as long as one of the frog's hops, how many additional hops will the frog make before Maria catches it?

49. The minute hand and the hour hand of a clock are in line with each other but pointing oppositely at 6:00 A.M. or 6:00 P.M. How many times do they cross each other between those two times?

50. Find two numbers whose product is one million. The numbers, however, cannot have any zeros in them when they are written in ordinary Hindu-Arabic decimal notation.

51. A Magic Hexagon
A hexagon has six sides that meet in six points called vertices (singular *vertex*). Brett wanted to make a mobile by hanging one of his designs from each side and each vertex of a hexagonal shape that was suspended from the middle. For the mobile to work, the weights on each of the six sides had to balance exactly; that is, the weight in the middle of one side and the two weights on the end of that side should total to the same amount as the similar combination of weights for any other side.

Brett had twelve different designs to hang. The smallest design weighed exactly one-twelfth of the largest design. Between those two designs, the weights were equally spaced, so that the next-to-smallest weighed twice the smallest design, the next largest weighed three times the smallest, and so forth.

How could Brett hang the designs to balance the mobile?

Hint: You can experiment by drawing a hexagon with circles at the vertices and in the middle of each side as shown below.

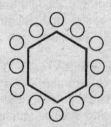

Assign each of the designs a number from one through twelve and try putting the numbers in the circles in various ways. If the numbers along each side of the hexagon (there are three numbers along each side) all add up to the same number, you will have solved the problem.

52. Whole Numbers and Almost-Perfect Squares

A number such as 3, 8, 15, 24, 35, or 48 is almost a perfect square, since each number is one less than a perfect square. This puzzle concerns the factors of such almost-perfect squares. Look at the whole-number factors of 3, 8, 24, 120 (one less than 11 squared), 360 (one less than 19 squared), and 960 (one less than 31 squared).

The whole-number factors of 3 are 1 and 3. The whole-number factors of 8 include 1 and 8. The whole-number factors of 24 include 3 and 8; of 120 include 120 and 1; of 360 include 120 and 3; and of 960 include 120 and 8. Thus, if you take the product of any two of the numbers 1, 3, 8, and 120, the result will be an almost-perfect square.

Your problem is to extend this list to include another whole number so that if you take the product of any two of the list of five numbers, the result will also be an almost-perfect square. In other words, your new list should include 1, 3, 8, 120, and some additional number that produces a list of numbers with the same property.

53. Fill in the Signs

A common puzzle is to start with a set of numbers such as 1, 2, 3 and be asked to insert appropriate signs to obtain a specified number. For example, if the set is 1, 2, 3 and the required number is 6, two possible solutions are $1 + 2 + 3 = 6$ and $1 \times 2 \times 3 = 6$. Other possible numbers that can be reached, using just the $+$, $-$, and $\times$ signs include $1 - 2 + 3 = 2$ and $1 + 2 - 3 = 0$. If parentheses are allowed, you can obtain $1 + (2 \times 3) = 7$, $1 \times (2 + 3) = 5$, and $(1 + 2) \times 3 = 9$. In all cases, the order of the digits cannot be changed.

Use the set 1, 2, 3, 4, 5, 6, 7, 8, 9 to obtain 100. The rules are that you can only use the signs $+$, $-$, $\times$, and parentheses, and the order of the digits cannot be changed.

54. More Fill in the Signs

The same problem has some elegant solutions if you change the rules slightly. Again, here is a demonstration of the revised version using 1, 2, and 3. First of all, two numbers may be written together to form a number that has the value it would in the ordinary Hindu-Arabic decimal system of numeration. Thus, from 1, 2, and 3, you can get such results as $123 = 123$, $12 + 3 = 15$, $1 + 23 = 24$, $12 - 3 = 9$, $12 \times 3 = 36$, and so forth.

Since this allows many possibilities, however, the rules will be restricted to allow only the signs $+$ and $-$ between the numbers. Both $\times$ and the use of parentheses are banned. As before, the order of the original set of digits cannot be changed.

With this new set of rules, form 100 with the digits 1, 2, 3, 4, 5, 6, 7, 8, 9. Use only $+$ $-$ and combine digits to make numerals for larger numbers.

There are many solutions to this puzzle. If you get one, try to find another that uses fewer signs. The record for the least number of $+$ and $-$ signs used is three. Can you tie the record?

55. Try It Backward

If you follow the same rules as in Problem **54,** you can also form 100 from 9, 8, 7, 6, 5, 4, 3, 2, 1 (in that order). The record for this one involves a total of four + or − signs. How well can you do?

56. A Crazy Dinner Party

Mrs. Pincenez always gives very proper dinner parties. Her long table seats exactly twenty-four persons, so she always makes sure that she has twenty-four people to dinner. Before each dinner party, Mrs. Pincenez always spends the afternoon carefully working out a seating plan so that each person invited will not only have appropriate partners to each side but the person across from each person will be someone with mutual interests. The seating arrangements are then written in excellent handwriting on special place cards and put on the table in the proper places.

One night, however, everything went wrong. All the guests sat totally at random in the twenty-four places. As a result, everyone was in the wrong place.

Mrs. Pincenez decided to make the most of a bad situation by asking the butler and maids to move the cards. The butler, however, misunderstood. He and twenty-three maids simply picked up the twenty-four cards and marched around the table until the card the butler held was correct. At that point, the maids and the butler gave their cards to whomever they were behind.

Is it always possible for one of the other guests also to have the correct card? That is, if the butler stops at the right place, will two of the guests get the same card with their correct name?

57. Almost a Train Wreck

In algebra, you frequently meet problems in which two trains, airplanes, or runners start at the same time and meet or pass at another time, while you are to determine the distance traveled or some such unknown quantity. Here are a couple of problems of that kind that can be solved without using algebra.

Two trains have accidentally gotten on the same track. They are heading toward each other. The track is 893 kilometers long. Both trains leave their stations at the same time. One train is a passenger train traveling at a rate of 180 kilometers per hour, while the other train is a freight train traveling at a rate of 120 kilometers per hour. An alert agent realizes that they are on a collision course one minute before the coming collision and radios both trains to stop. How far apart are the two trains one minute before they would collide?

58. The Sister's Sheep

Two sisters inherited a herd of sheep when their father died. Since neither wanted the sheep, they sold the whole herd. By an odd coincidence, the price paid for each sheep was the same number of dollars as the number of sheep in the herd. The buyer paid the sisters in ten-dollar bills. Since the total purchase price was not a multiple of ten, the buyer paid the additional amount in silver dollars.

The older sister began to count out the money, giving herself the first bill, her younger sister the next, and so forth. At the end of the count, the older sister also got the last ten-dollar bill. The younger sister complained that the division was not fair, so the older one gave the younger all the silver dollars. The younger one still did not have an equal share, so the older sister opened her purse and gave her sister some dollar bills. How many dollar bills did the older sister give the younger one?

This problem looks unsolvable, because you do not have very much information. Surprisingly, however, it can be solved.

Hint: You do not need to know the number of sheep or the purchase price to solve the problem.

Fun with Geometry

59. Cutting a Fine Figure

Just as there are many interesting mathematical problems about numbers, there are also problems and surprises concerning shapes. People have been amusing themselves with shapes since before the ancient Greeks worked out geometry in detail.

One set of problems consists of creating one shape from another. If you have ever played tangrams, then you know something of the complexity involved. In tangrams, however, you always work with the same basic seven shapes. Did you ever think how much easier the tangram problems would be if you could choose the shapes as you go along?

It turns out not to be so easy, however. Consider this problem: Starting with three equal squares, cut them into nine pieces that can be reformed to make a single square with the same area as the combined areas of the three given squares.

Since this is not easy, here are a few clues. One small square is not cut at all. If you cut the other two squares once, each in the same (right) way, and try to use the pieces to get close to the large square, you may be able to see which four other cuts need to be made to complete the job. It may help to calculate the area of the large square and then draw it, so that you can assemble the pieces on the drawing.

60. Three-Dimensional Tangrams

The inventive Piet Hein discovered a suitable three-dimensional version of tangrams. As in tangrams, there are seven pieces. These pieces can be assembled into a cube, just as the tans can be assembled into a square. Also, Piet Hein's pieces, which he calls Soma pieces, can be used to form all sorts of three-dimensional forms, such as step pyramids, chairs, sofas, and beds.

The seven Soma pieces are shown on page 64. All of them, except for A, are formed from four identical cubes, while A is formed from three identical cubes. You can make a set of Soma cubes by gluing twenty-seven children's blocks together.

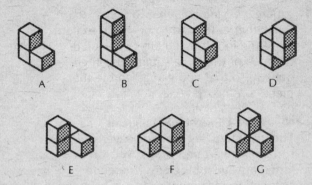

A B C D

E F G

There is a simple rule that describes the construction of the pieces. Your challenge is to find it. The rule describes all of the Soma pieces but does not include any other shapes. If you make the Soma pieces, you should be able to show that they can be assembled to form a cube.

61. Triangles

The figure shown below is made from six line segments of the same length. How many triangles are formed by the six line segments?

Notice that all the triangles have the same shape. In fact, all of them are equilateral triangles. Equilateral triangles have three sides and three angles of the same size.

Find a different figure that produces the same number of equilateral triangles and that is also made from exactly six line segments of the same length.

62. The Bridge of Tran-Slate Way

The towns of Tran and Slate are on either side of a giant, straight canyon. After many years, the towns decided to build a road between them. Since the land between the towns was flat except for the canyon, the road could be perfectly straight—except for the canyon. The canyon needed to be bridged, and the least expensive way would be to make the bridge perpendicular to the canyon walls. But a straight road from one town to the other would not meet the canyon at a place where the shortest possible bridge could be built. That is, a straight road between the towns would require a bridge that was not perpendicular to the sides of the canyon. Where was the best place to put the bridge to make both the road and the bridge as short as possible? (*See* illustration and hint, p. 66)

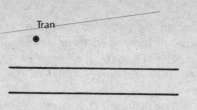

Tran

Slate

Hint: Begin by assuming that you have solved the problem. And remember that the shortest distance between two points is a straight line.

63. Professor Rosseforp's Garden

Professor Rosseforp, the noted absent-minded mathematician, was also an enthusiastic amateur herb gardener. One day, he called the garden supply store to order some fertilizer. Bob, the man at the garden store, asked how much area the professor needed to cover.

"Gosh," said the professor. "I forgot to measure the garden. I'll measure it this afternoon and let you know the area of the herb garden. One of my students lives near the store, and I'll send the information with her."

Later that afternoon, the student dropped off the note at the garden store. Bob was not surprised to find that, although the professor had measured the garden, he had forgotten to say in the note what the area was. In fact, all the note showed was the following drawing.

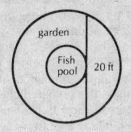

After a few moments of being puzzled, Bob suddenly figured out the area of Professor Rosseforp's herb garden. Can you?

64. The Long Dive
The Cheevers have a rectangular swimming pool that has a circular fence around it.

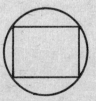

One day their nephew Jack was swimming in the pool. He dived from the board in the middle of one of the short sides of the rectangle to the exact middle of the pool. He was so excited, he wanted to know exactly how far he had dived.

Mr. Cheever did not have a measuring tool handy, but he knew that the pool was nine feet deep at one end and six feet deep at the other. He used the two depths to measure points on a long pole he kept for cleaning the bottom of the pool. Then he used the pole, which turned out to be too short to measure the distance Jack had dived, to measure the distances shown below.

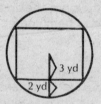

Then Mr. Cheever made Jack figure out how far he had dived. Can you do it also?

65. The Bear and the Bird

There is an old puzzle about a bear, which you may have heard. A bear walks one mile south, one mile east, and one mile north. At that point, the bear is back where it started. What color is the bear?

Here is a related puzzle that is a bit harder. A bird walks one mile south, one mile east, and one mile north. At that point, the bird is back where it started from. What color is the bird?

No answer will be accepted without a complete explanation.

Hint: Certain birds and animals are found only in certain locations in the world.

66. The Patchwork Quilt

Mr. Darcy was very fond of a patchwork quilt that he had received from his grandmother. It was a rectangle nine squares by twelve squares (or 108 squares in all).

One day, to his horror, Mr. Darcy spilled a bottle of indelible ink right in the middle of the quilt. The bottle had tipped over, throwing the ink along eight of the squares in a line in the middle of the quilt.

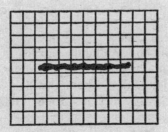

No cleaning fluid Mr. Darcy used removed the ink. In fact, each thing he tried made the stains worse and even began to dissolve parts of the cloth. Finally, he took the quilt to his local dry cleaners.

The person who ran the dry cleaners told Mr. Darcy that nothing could be done to fix the damaged squares. "But," she said, "if you would be satisfied with a ten-by-ten quilt, I can cut the quilt into two pieces and put it back together to form a square."

Mr. Darcy, who had thought of cutting all the squares apart and sewing them together (but was appalled by the amount of work involved) was delighted with the dry cleaner's solution to the problem.

How can you cut the quilt apart (along the edges of the squares) into exactly two pieces with the damaged squares removed so that the two pieces can then be sewn together to make a square quilt?

67. In Taxicab Circles

Max drove a cab for a living, but his hobby was mathematics. Therefore, he had noticed certain mathematical facts about the city in which he drove. It had been laid out so that every city block was an exact square, with twelve blocks making up exactly one mile. Therefore, if two corner locations were not on the same street, there were several ways to drive from one corner to the other that were all the same length. For example, if one corner was Fifth Avenue and D Street while the other corner was Seventh Avenue and G Street, the distance was the same whether Max drove from Fifth and D along the avenue to G Street and then over to Seventh or if he drove along D to Seventh and then over to G. In fact, there were eight other paths of the same length that he could follow, twisting and turning as the lights changed so that he could make the same length trip in the shortest possible time.

One day a pair of lovers got in Max's cab and told him to drive in a circle. When Max pointed out the No U-turn sign, the young man in the back seat said, "No, a big circle—with a radius of a mile."

Max observed that they were just twelve blocks from the corner of Twelfth Avenue and L Street and then proceeded to drive so that his path was one of the many shortest possible that took the cab to all corners that were exactly twelve blocks from the corner of Twelfth and L.

If you adopt Max's definition of a taxicab circle, how far did he drive if he made exactly one trip around the taxicab circle? Also, what is the value of pi (the ratio of the taxicab circle's circumference to its diameter)? Describe the taxicab circle in terms of ordinary geometry.

68. Loretta Chooses a Room

Loretta was going to be a senior in college, majoring in mathematics. Finally, she had drawn a low number in the college housing lottery, so she was sure of getting her first choice of the building in which she wanted to live.

Rooms were available in every one of the forty houses along College Row. All of her friends—Alice, Bryan, Catherine, Diana, Ed, Faye, George, Hattie, Irma, Jack, and Kathleen—were planning to live on College Row and had already selected the buildings where they would live. Loretta drew a sketch of how her friends had arranged themselves.

A B   C D   E F   G H I J   K

Loretta knew that she would be visiting all of her friends frequently during the year. She decided that she wanted to live where the distance she would have to travel to do this would be a minimum. In other words, she wanted to choose the building so that the sum of the distances from her building to the buildings where her friends lived would be a minimum. Where along College Row should she live?

69. Put Your Two Yen In

The Japanese, as you probably know, use the yen as a monetary unit. What you may not know is that one yen is a coin, not a bill. In fact, it is an extremely handy coin. One yen is exactly one gram in mass, so a supply of one-yen coins can be used with a balance scale to weigh small objects in grams. The diameter of the one-yen coin is exactly two centimeters, so it is also possible to use the coin to measure lengths in centimeters.

If you have a couple of handfuls of one-yen coins you can use them to mark off a length on a line that is exactly a whole number of centimeters. It is easy to see how you could mark off the distance if the distance is an even number of centimeters. How could you use your one-yen coins to mark off a length that is exactly an odd number of centimeters?

You can assume that you have a straightedge that you use to draw the line in the first place. You are also allowed to use the straightedge in marking off the distance.

Fun with Paradoxes

70. The Liar

A paradox in mathematics is a result or statement with an internal contradiction as well as a result or statement that goes strongly against intuition.

For example, the paradox "This statement is false" is called *The Liar*. It is a contradiction because if The Liar is true, then it's false; but if it is false, then it's true.

You rule this kind of paradox out of mathematics by saying that you cannot use a sentence that talks about itself. Such sentences are neither true nor false. Even a sentence such as "This sentence is in English" talks about itself, so it must be declared off limits. Can you give a good reason why "This sentence is in English" should not be declared true?

If you allow sentences that talk about themselves to be either true or false, some very strange contradictions could arise. For example, there is a sentence in English that would have to be counted as true, but the negation of that sentence would also have to be counted as true. Can you find what those sentences are?

71. Finding the Least Number

All whole numbers can be named in English in more than one way. For example, the same number can easily be recognized as twenty-five, the square of five, the cube root of one hundred twenty-five, and the square of the third prime.

Sometimes, the shortest way to name a number in English is shorter than the common English name for the number; for example, *the first prime on an alphabetical list in English names* takes fifty-six letters and spaces to write, but the name of that prime in English is *eight billion eighteen million eighteen thousand eight hundred fifty-one,* which takes seventy-two letters and spaces. (Count the hyphen as a letter or space.) Similarly, *the last prime on an alphabetical list in English names* is fifty-five letters and spaces long, while the name of the prime is *two vingintillion two undecillion two trillion two thousand two hundred ninety-three,* which contains eighty-four letters and spaces.

Assume that you can always find the shortest name in English for each whole number, even if it is merely the common name in English. Clearly, every number will have a name. Some numbers will have names that are shorter than a hundred letters and spaces long. Others, especially as you get to larger numbers, may have no names that are shorter than a hundred letters or spaces. It is, in fact, easy to show that the number of names that are possible that are shorter than a hundred letters or spaces is finite. Since the set of whole numbers is infinite, there must be some that have names longer than a hundred letters and spaces.

Therefore, just as you can find the first prime on a list in alphabetical order, you should be able to find *the least number that cannot be named in a hundred letters and spaces or fewer*. In fact, however, this number cannot be named. Why not?

Hint: You can count on this being a trick question, since it is in the section on paradoxes. So, count on it.

72. A Way Around the Square
If you measure the length of one side of a square in centimeters, the perimeter and the area of the square can be found. For most squares, the perimeter will be a different number from area. It is possible, however, to choose a unit so that the area of the square will be the same

as the perimeter. Can you describe how to choose such a unit?

73. Another Way to Square the Circle

Consider a circle of diameter d. From the formula for the circumference of a circle, $C = \pi d$, and the formula for the area, $A = \pi r^2$, you can calculate the ratio of the circumference to the area. Substitute $d/2$ for r in the area formula, and you get $A = \frac{1}{4} \pi d^2$. The ratio of C/A is then simply $4/d$, since some things cancel.

Similarly, consider a square whose edge is d. Its perimeter is $4d$, while its area is d^2. Again, if you find the ratio of perimeter to area, some things cancel, so $P/A = 4/d$.

This argument shows that the ratio of the distance around a circle to its area is the same as the ratio of a distance around a square to its area. In other words, if you took a string and tied its ends together, you would be able to enclose the same area by forming a circle or by forming a square with the string.

If that is true, then you can square the circle (that is, find a square with the same area as a given circle) merely by constructing a square on the diameter of the circle. However, it is known that the circle cannot be squared with a straightedge and compasses. What is wrong with the argument?

74. A Small Budget of Paradoxes

In what follows, there are no puzzles to be solved, so no answers are provided. These are just a few short paradoxes for you to think about, demonstrating that logic has a few twists in it.

The Greeks thought of this one. A lawyer named Protagoras also taught law for a fee. He advertised his skills as a teacher by offering his students a contract that states that they do not have to pay him until they have won their first case. If the student loses the first case, the student does not have to pay Protagoras at all.

One student of Protagoras', however, sees a loophole. After taking the course, the student avoids arguing any cases. Since the student has not won the first case, the student escapes the fee for the course. Protagoras feels cheated, so he sues the student for his fee. When the case comes to trial, the student represents himself.

If the student loses the case, then, by terms of their original agreement, there is no fee for the course. If the student wins the case, however, then, since it is the student's first case, there will be a fee. (But, of course, winning the case means that the student does not have to pay a fee, while losing it means that the fee must be paid.)

75. Words That Talk About Themselves

If you have read the earlier part of this book, then you have met both numbers and sentences that tell something about themselves. Words can also talk about themselves. For example, the word *short* is short and the word *polysyllabic* is polysyllabic. On the other hand, *red* is not red (in this book at least), and *long* is not a long word.

For the most part, words do not describe themselves, so let us call words such as *red* and *long* **normal**. On the other hand, we could call words that do talk about themselves, such as *short* or *polysyllabic*, **abnormal**.

Using this scheme, then, you can classify words:

	Normal	Abnormal
monosyllabic	X	
inexpensive	X	
English		X
French	X	
elephant	X	
abnormal	X	
normal	?	?

If the word *normal* describes itself, then it is abnormal. But that does not make sense, since the word *normal* does not describe a word that is abnormal.

But if *normal* does not talk about itself, then it is normal, in which case the word *normal* does describe itself.

76. Life in Mayor City

The state legislature noticed that problems were caused by some cities having no mayors, while in other cities that had mayors, the mayor lived outside the city. So the legislature passed a law that every city must have a mayor and that the mayor must live in the city.

One of the legislators, however, argued that it might not always be possible for every mayor to live in the city of which he or she was mayor, but having two mayors in the same city might confuse people. Therefore, he proposed an amendment to the law setting up a special Mayor City where mayors who lived outside the city of which they were mayor must live. The only residents of Mayor City would be mayors that lived outside of the city they governed. This amendment also passed.

As a result the law became that either the mayor must live in the city of which he or she is mayor, or else the mayor must live in Mayor City; and all cities must have a mayor.

A problem soon developed with the law. Since Mayor City is a city, it had to have a mayor. Where should the mayor of Mayor City live?

77. Achilles and the Tortoise

Last, the most famous paradox of them all. This is one of the famous paradoxes of Zeno of Elea, first proposed around 450 B.C., and a source of discussion ever since.

Achilles was a Greek warrior who was also famous as a very fast runner. A tortoise is a very slow-moving animal. Therefore, in a race between Achilles and a tortoise, you would expect Achilles to win even if the tortoise had a head start.

Zeno argued, however, that the tortoise would always win a race if the tortoise had a head start. Here is the way it works.

The tortoise has a head start. In the first part of the race, Achilles must run until he reaches the point where the tortoise started. But, during that same time, the tortoise will have moved on to a new point. Now you are in the same situation as before, with the tortoise having a new head start over Achilles. Therefore, in the second part of the race, Achilles must reach the point where the tortoise was, but finds that when he gets there, the tortoise has again moved on. Clearly, the same situation will repeat itself indefinitely. The tortoise will win the race.

Answers

1. Slide the bottom toothpick in the base of the glass half its distance to the right. Pick up the toothpick that forms the left-hand side of the glass and move it to be perpendicular to the right-hand end of the toothpick you previously moved. The "glass" is now upside down, and the coin has been removed.

2. Remove the two toothpicks shown by dashed lines.

3. Here is the solution for the easier problem in the hint. The dashed lines show the original positions of the coins. The arrows show the moves to the new positions.

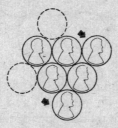

The original problem can be solved in much the same way.

4. Number the drums (or coins) as shown below.

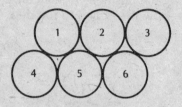

Move the drum numbered 3 so that it touches drums numbered 4 and 5. Then slide the drum numbered 5 out of the center. Be sure drum 5 continues to touch drum 3 (or 6) while you hold drums 5 and 6 (or 3) steady as you slip inside the circle. Then pull drum 5 toward you to close the circle as shown.

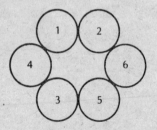

Note: Another solution is possible.

5. For the lock with eight buttons, move button 4 to 7, 6 to 2, 1 to 3, and 5 to 8.

6. When the lock has ten buttons, you double the buttons at one end by moving 7 to 10. Then the remaining buttons are the same as in the problem with eight buttons.

7. The garden borders are shown as dashed lines.

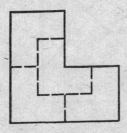

8. Often people add the unnecessary fourth rule that all the line segments have to be inside the square formed by the dots. The solution, however, involves going outside that square.

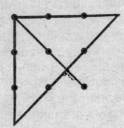

9. The path you take and where you start is more important in connecting sixteen dots than it is in connecting nine, so small arrowheads are used to show the complete solution.

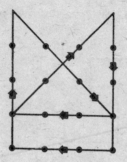

10. Put two parallel rows of coins on a blank sheet of paper, like the top and bottom of a nine-dot square. Mark their positions. Now use the centers of these coins as the points of a six-pointed star made by the opposite corners to each other and the middle coin in each row to the opposite corners. Place the other three coins where the two lines joining the opposite corners meet, and at the two places where the lines from opposite middle coins meet. The six lines that make up the star form six of the required straight rows of three trees.

The dashed lines are inserted to show the other four straight rows of three trees.

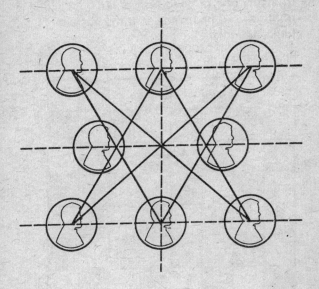

11. You may have an answer that looks different than the one shown below. For one thing, you can look at the board from any one of its four sides. Try rotating your board to see if the answer looks like this.

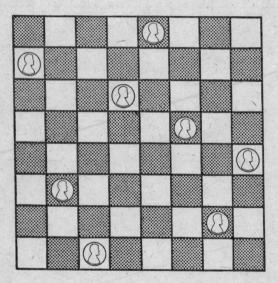

It may still not be the same. The mirror images of this solution are also solutions. Furthermore, there are eleven totally different solutions, plus their rotations and mirror images. If you got another answer, and if it meets the rules of the problem, then you have a right answer.

If you want a real challenge, try to find the other solutions that are not simply rotations or mirror images of each other. Remember that there are twelve fundamentally different solutions in all.

12.   The answer for the rooks is the same as for the queens; a maximum of eight rooks can be placed on the board so that no one of them can attack another. Since each rook controls one row and one column, it is easy to see that the maximum would have to be eight. There are many different possible solutions for eight rooks (5282, in fact), but the easiest is to place the eight rooks along the longest diagonal of the board.

13.   As it says in the hint, each knight must always attack a different color from the one that it is resting on. Therefore, if you put as many knights as you can on one of the colors, then none of them can attack another. But if you added one knight on the other color, it could be attacked no matter where it is. Therefore, the answer is that thirty-two knights (the number of squares of one color) is the maximum number that can be put on the board so that none of them can attack another. There are exactly two ways to do this.

14. Arrange the toothpicks as shown below.

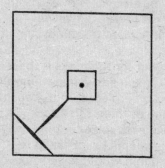

If you know the Pythagorean Theorem, you can solve this using mathematics instead of a model. The distance from the corner of the pool to the corner of the island is about 5.66 meters. The planks are each almost 4 meters long. When one plank is placed along a corner of the pool, the midpoint of the plank will reach about 2 meters from the corner. Since $4 + 2 = 6$ is greater than 5.66, the method will work even if the planks are slightly shorter than 4 meters each (4 meters is the shortest distance from the island to the side of the pool).

15. Since the baker replied to Mrs. Cook, it is clear that Mrs. Cook is not the baker. Therefore, the baker must be either Mr. Farmer or Miss Baker. Since no names match the job, the baker is Mr. Farmer. From this, it is clear that Mrs. Cook must be either the cook or the farmer. Since she cannot be the cook, she is the farmer. Miss Baker is the cook.

16. Terry.

Notice that rule (1) implies that if Don stocks shelves, then Cynthia bags groceries. By rule (2), if Don stocks shelves, then Terry bags groceries. But by rule (3), Terry and Cynthia cannot both bag groceries. Therefore, Don cannot stock shelves, or the whole system breaks down. Then, by rule (1), Cynthia must *always* stock shelves. Every day, then, Cynthia stocks shelves and Don bags groceries. Neither of them could have stocked shelves one day and bagged groceries the next. Terry, however, can do either. The rules do not specify what job is assigned to Terry, so it is possible to stock shelves one day and bag groceries the next.

17.   Shakespeare was a clever writer.

The analysis is as follows: By combining (3) and (5), you get "Shakespeare was a true poet." By combining this result with (2), you get "Shakespeare can stir the hearts of men." By combining this result with (4) you get "Shakespeare understands human nature." And, finally, by combining this result with (1), you obtain "Shakespeare was a clever writer."

18.   I avoid kangaroos.

The analysis is as follows: Combine (3) and (9) to obtain "I avoid animals that do not take to me." Combine this result with (6) to get "I avoid animals that are not in this house." Combine this with (1) to get "I avoid animals that are not cats." Combine this with (5) to get "I avoid animals that do not kill mice." Combine this with (8) to get "I avoid animals that are not carnivores." Combine this with (4) to get "I avoid animals that do not prowl at night." Combine this with (10) to get "I avoid animals that do not gaze at the moon." Combine this with (2) to get "I avoid animals that are not suitable for pets." Finally, combine this with (7) to obtain "I avoid kangaroos."

19. Since each bag is mislabeled, look at one document from the bag marked "letters and secrets." If an ordinary letter is drawn, then the bag marked "secrets" cannot contain only secrets, so it must contain both letters and secrets. Take the bag labeled letters. The diagram shows the possibilities.

Label on Bag	Actual Contents	Label on Bag	Actual Contents
letters and secrets	letters	letters and secrets	secrets
letters	secrets	letters	both
secrets	both	secrets	letters

20. The four weights are 1 gram, 3 grams, 9 grams, and 27 grams. The first few combinations are:

Amount to be Weighed in Left-Hand Pan	Weight in Left-Hand Pan	Weight in Right-Hand Pan
1	0	1
2	1	3
3	0	3
4	0	1,3
5	1,3	9
6	3	9
7	3	9,1
8	1	9
9	0	9
10	0	9,1
11	1	9,3
12	0	9,3
13	0	9,3,1
14	9,3,1	27

and so forth. Since $1 + 3 + 9 + 27 = 40$, that is the maximum amount that can be weighed by this method.

21. The first day, put six coins on each side of the balance scale. Remember the dates on the six heavier coins. The second day, put three coins from the six whose dates you have remembered on each side of the balance scale. Remember the dates on the three heavier coins. The third day, take two of the coins for which you have memorized the dates and place one on each side of the balance. If one of them is heavier, it is the fake coin. If not, the remaining coin, whose date you have remembered, is the fake.

22. To always obtain a draw at Toe Tac Tic, after putting the X in the center, counter each move the O's make with an X that is symmetrically opposite the O with respect to the center X. For example, if the first O move is the lower left square, the symmetrical move would be the upper right square. If the first move is the upper middle square, the symmetrical move is the bottom middle square.

23. No problem asked. However, control of the center frequently leads to a win.

24. The winning strategies for the first player in Tac Tix are as follows: Either take the center counter, one of the corner counters, or all of a central row or column. If you take a central row or column, you can play symmetrically against the second player, taking as many counters from the same row or column as that player does, but on the opposite side of the center line—making sure that your last move leaves the second player with only a single counter.

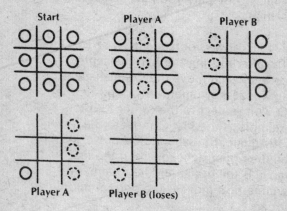

Start   Player A   Player B

Player A   Player B (loses)

25.   The arrangement of the nine HOT cards in the Tic Tac Toe diagram will be either the image shown or one that is basically the same (that is, a mirror image or upside down).

HOT   FORM   WOES

TANK   HEAR   WASP

TIES   BRIM   SHIP

With this arrangement, it is clear that choosing a HOT card is equivalent to marking an X or O in a square of Tic Tac Toe. As with Tic Tac Toe, the game will always end in a draw if the first player chooses HEAR and both players thereafter make the best moves. Against an inexperienced HOT player, however, the best strategy is to take either HOT, WOES, TIED, or SHIP on the first move, hoping that the other player will not take HEAR.

26. One of the nice things about this game is that there is no way of knowing for sure that you have found the least possible number of moves. It is entirely possible that you can find a solution in six moves, or even fewer. Here is how to get from *girl* to *boy* in seven moves.

GIRL
GILL
BILL
BOLL
BOLT
BOAT
BOA
BOY

27. With two players, the first player should begin with Maine. No state name begins with E or ends with M. You also can win by starting with Kentucky since this forces the second player to use New York, and you can finish with Michigan (or Washington or Wisconsin). You can find some other winning strategies on your own.

With three players, the strategy is to knock out the third player first. If you eliminate the second player, the third player can win using Maine. If the third player is the first to be out, then you can use Maine to get rid of the second player and win. Therefore, your first move should be Tennessee. This forces the second player to name either Connecticut or Vermont, each of which eliminates the third player. Now you can use Maine, Kentucky, or one of the combinations you found on your own.

28.   If one player completely blocks the other player, the player doing the blocking will have completed a chain, winning the game. If one player does not completely block the other player, the other player can win. In either case, there is no draw possible.

In four-by-four Hex, the four middle positions, marked with X's on the board shown below, guarantee a win for the first player to mark one of them.

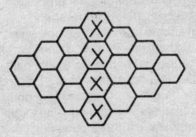

29. No problem asked.

30. When the three sailors reached the island, there were 15 coconuts.

One approach to solving the puzzle is to look at an easier problem. Suppose the captain took exactly half, the midshipman took exactly half of what was remaining, and the swab took exactly half of the remaining coconuts, but there was one coconut left for the monkey. Then the swab must have taken one coconut (half of two is one, leaving one), the midshipman must have taken two coconuts to have left two, and the captain must have taken four cocounts to have left four. Therefore, the total for the easier problem is $4 + 2 + 1 + 1$, or 8.

Now go back to the original problem. It should be clear that odd numbers must be available at each step, not even numbers. If there were three coconuts available to the swab, he could take half that number (1½ coconuts) plus a half coconut (for a total of two), leaving one for the monkey. Now work your way up. The midshipman left three coconuts for the sailor, so he must have taken four, and the total number available to him was seven. Similarly, since the captain left seven for the midshipman, he must have taken eight. $8 + 4 + 2 + 1 = 15$.

31.   The one remaining in the case of *One Potato* played with seven persons will be the first one counted. Therefore, the best place to stand is at A. In this case, it does not matter whether the counting takes place clockwise or counterclockwise.

32.   Josephus arranged himself to stand at position 16 while his friend was put at position 31.

33.   Here is how the stepmother arranged the children.

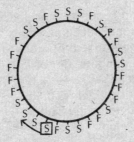

The mathematical F should stand at position 23, if the position where counting begins is numbered 1 and the count proceeds initially in the order of increasing numbers. When the counting is reversed, all the S's are eliminated, so the mathematical F becomes the heir.

34. If you divide 50 by ½ and add 3, the answer is 103. For some reason, a lot of people answer 28, which is 50 times ½ plus 3.

35. The errors are (B), which should be 10.394, and (E), which should be $^{19}/_{51}$, and the statement that says that there are three errors for you to detect. (Of course, counting that statement makes the assertion true, so there are only two errors, in which case the statement is false.)

36. There is no sum in which a and c are different and b can be canceled. Intuitively, you may recognize that adding the same nonzero number to the numerator and denominator of a fraction always changes its value. Here is a way to show that using algebra. If you multiply $^a/_c$ by $b + c$, the result is

$a + b = (^a/_c) (b + c)$
$a + b = (^a/_c) b + a$

so

$b = (^a/_c) b$

But the conditions of the problem were that a and c were not equal and b was not 0. Since $^a/_c$ cannot be 1 and b cannot be 0, this last equation cannot be true.

The student's fallacy with $^{16}\!/_{64}$ looks superficially similar, but the student was working on 10 + 6 over 60 + 4, so the student was not even canceling the same number. The proof that you cannot cancel in sums in the numerator and denominator does not apply since the sums in $^{16}\!/_{64}$ are of the form

$$\frac{(a + b)}{(c + d)}$$

where a, b, c, and d are all different numbers. In this case, there are combinations in which you can remove an addend from the numerator and a different addend from the denominator to get the correctly simplified fraction. The example you were asked to find is $^{19}\!/_{95}$.

37. They would have finished fifteen minutes earlier at 3:45 P.M.

Since the amount of crumpled paper doubles each time, the original 4:00 P.M. finish means that the room was half full of paper at 3:45. If Fred had started with two sheets of paper instead of one, the amount at each fifteen-minute tossing would be double what it was in actuality. Therefore, if Fred began with two sheets, the room would have been full by 3:45 instead of by 4:00.

38. 1885.

The birth year must be a counting number, so look at multiples of 29. While a grandmother can be any age over 30 or so, it seems reasonable to start testing multiples around the age of 60. You will find that $60 \times 29 = 1740$, which is clearly too small, while 70×29 is 2030, which is clearly too large. The right answer is $65 \times 29 = 1885$, since a person born in 1885 would be 65 in 1950.

39. 1892.

Again, you make some assumptions. Mr. Oleander's birthdate is most likely near Mrs. Oleander's. Since the year must be a counting number, you need to find perfect squares that are somewhere near 1885. You can find that 45 squared is 2025, which is clearly too large. Similarly, 43 squared, or 1849, is too small to be likely, since that would mean that Mr. Oleander was 58 when he married a child bride of 16 and 108 in 1950, which has to be ruled out since he is still alive in a year that is clearly later than 1950. Therefore, the correct square is 44 squared, or 1892. In fact, Mrs. Oleander was seven years older than her husband.

40. Mr. Oleander was 48 and his nine children were 2, 5, 8, 11, 14, 17, 20, 23, and 26.

Probably the best way to solve this is simply by trial and error. You need to find nine numbers that are equally spaced whose sum of squares is also a perfect square. It is a good idea to have a calculator with which to work. The sum of the squares from one through nine is only 276, so it is clear that you will need larger numbers (and probably a larger interval) since the square root of 276 is about sixteen. Doubling the interval from one to two years produces ages of 1, 3, 5, 7, 9, 11, 13, 15, and 17. The sum of the squares of these numbers is 969, whose square root is around thirty-one (although 969 is not a perfect square). Since a 31-year-old father *might* have a 17-year-old child—although it is unlikely—it is clear that the intervals must be two or three years between children, not one. Try three years, giving 1, 4, 7, 10, 13, 16, 19, 22, and 25 as the ages of the children. The sum of the squares of these numbers is 2073, whose square root is near forty-five. Now we are getting close, although 2073 is not a perfect square. However, shifting all the ages up one year produces a sum of 2304, which is exactly the square of forty-eight, giving the answer. That Mrs. Oleander was 55 when her last child was born is just another remarkable fact about this family.

41.   9:11:30

There are two ways to solve this, with what mathematicians call "brute force" or by reasoning out the problem. Here is the brute force solution: The total number of handshakes is 276, which is the number of combinations of twenty-four things taken two at a time. If you know the formula, it is the 24! divided by the product of 2! times 22!. (24! is 24 × 23 × 22 × . . . × 3 × 2 × 1.) If you do not know the formula, you can work out the number of handshakes by drawing a polygon with twenty-four sides, then drawing all of the diagonals. The sum of the number of diagonals and the number of sides will be the number of handshakes, or 276. It may help to start with a triangle or square and work your way up to a twenty-four-sided figure, keeping track of the sum of the number of diagonals and the number of sides in a table, while looking for a pattern. From the total number of handshakes you can divide by twelve to get the number of thirty-second periods, which is twenty-three. Half of twenty-three is the number of minutes that elapse during the handshaking period.

There is an easier way, however. Pretend that you are at the conference. You will shake hands with twenty-three other people there, each handshake taking thirty seconds. When you have finished all your handshakes, so will everyone else. It will be 9:11:30.

42. 2:30 P.M.

Since it took Emily twelve minutes to saw a log into three pieces, she made one cut per six minutes of sawing. There are two cuts required for three pieces, and three cuts required for four pieces. Therefore, the second log took eighteen minutes. $12 + 18 = 30$.

It is easy to mistakenly think that three pieces will take four minutes per piece, so that four pieces will take sixteen minutes, instead of eighteen minutes. The essential idea involved is to count cuts, not pieces, however.

43. 106 poems.

From midnight to 3:30 A.M. is 210 minutes, so Elroy set 210 digits. The first nine poems required nine digits. Thereafter, the next ninety poems, if there are that many, require two digits each. That would make 189 digits, which is not enough. The next 900 poems would require three minutes to set the three digits in each page number, but clearly there are not that many more poems. Subtract 189 from 210 to obtain twenty-one. The number of minutes required for the three-digit page numbers is twenty-one, so the number of three-digit page numbers is seven. 99 + 7 = 106.

44. Boy's style: twenty-one right-handed gloves and two left-handed gloves. Girl's style: twenty-three right-handed gloves and four left-handed gloves.

This problem can be solved by making a table of the facts you know, then using arithmetic to find the rest of the facts.

	Left	Right	Total
Girls	4	?	?
Boys	?		23
TOTAL	?	44	50

It is easy to find the total number of left-handers by subtracting forty-four from fifty and the total number of girls by subtracting twenty-three from fifty. Then you have two numbers and one ? in each row and column, so you can complete the solution.

45. Yes.

This problem can be solved the same way as the other, except it is easier to make two tables.

	Boys	Girls	Total
Grade 7	12	?	22
Grade 8	?	17	?
TOTAL	?	?	48

	Boys	Girls	Total
Softball	12	?	?
Track	?	14	?
TOTAL	?	?	48

From the first table, you can see that the number of eighth-grade students in all is twenty-six. This gives you enough information to determine the total of eighth-grade boys, nine, all of whom want track. Now you have enough information to find the total number who want track, which is the 14 + 9, or 23. You can subtract this result from forty-eight to find the total number who want softball, which is twenty-five. Since twelve boys want softball, so do thirteen girls, enough for a team.

46. 10.

If you number the committees and give the Senators letters, you can construct a table. Start off with committee 1 having just two members, A and B. This would not work, since committee 2 would have B and C, and committee 3 would have to have C and A. Since A, B, and C are now all on two committees each, there are no Senators available for committee 4 to overlap with the membership of committee 3. A similar analysis will show that if A, B, and C are on committee 1, there will be no way to meet the conditions.

You can, however, meet the conditions with four members to a committee as follows.

```
committee 1:   A,  B,  C,  D
committee 2:   A,          E,  F,  G
committee 3:       B,      E,          H,  I
committee 4:           C,      F,      H,     J
committee 5:               D,      G,      I, J
```

Each member is on exactly two committees. Each pair of committees has exactly one member in common. If you added another Senator, K, K would have to be on two committees—in which case, those two committees would have two members in common, so you have to stop at ten members.

47. 20 cats and 10 canaries.

Suppose all the pets were cats. Then thirty cats need thirty hats and 120 shoes; but there are only fifty pairs, or 100 shoes, ordered. Now trade enough cats for canaries to reduce the number of shoes from 120 to 100. Since each canary requires just one pair of shoes, twenty shoes mean ten canaries. If there are ten canaries, there can only be twenty cats.

48. 30 hops.

Measure the whole problem in frog hops per a unit of time that is the time for three hops. Maria travels four frog hops while the frog travels three in one unit of time. However, the frog has a ten-hop headstart. At the end of the first unit of time, the frog is thirteen hops from the starting place, while Maria is four hops away from the starting place, so the distance between them is nine hops. Similarly, Maria will get one frog hop closer in each unit of time, so she will catch the frog after ten units of time. In ten units of time, the frog will make thirty hops.

49. 11 times.

The times are approximately 6:30, 7:35, 8:40, 9:45, 10:55, 12:00, 1:05, 2:10, 3:15, 4:20, and 5:30.

50. 15,525 and 64.

Since ten and five are the only factors of ten, they are also the only prime factors of 1,000,000. Therefore, the only pair of factors whose product is 1,000,000 that do not have any zeros in the numeral is found by separating the two's from the five's. Since there are six factors of two and of five in 1,000,000, the required factors are the sixth powers of two and five, or 64 and 15,525.

51. The designs should be placed as shown below.

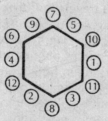

This problem is made harder because you do not know what the total for a side is to be. Start by thinking that the number has to be greater than 6 (because $1 + 2 + 3 = 6$) and less than 33 (because $10 + 11 + 12 = 33$). Halfway between these extremes is 19.5, so the magic sum should be somewhere near 20. Also notice that $1 + 2 + 3 + \ldots + 12 = 78$, but all the numbers at the vertices will be added twice, since they are each along two different sides, so the magic sum must be greater than $78 \div 12$, or 13. On the other hand, it cannot be as great as 26, since not all of the numbers are used twice. Halfway between 26 and 13 is also 19.5, which also suggests that 20 might be the magic sum. However, if you try 20, you will find that it does not work.

A little thought will show that the magic sum will be an even number. If it were odd, there would have to be either three odd numbers along a side or just one. This can be accomplished, but there is no way to add the three odd numbers along the two sides to produce the same sum. If one group of three numbers adds, for example, to 21, the other adds to 15. The magic sum is most likely to be either 18 or 22. It turns out to be 22.

52.   0. The new list of 0, 1, 3, 8, 120 has the property because 0 times any number is 0, and 0 is by definition an almost-perfect square. If you had trouble with this one, it was probably because you

were looking for a *counting number* that can be added to the list. Although the somewhat misleading introduction to the problem suggests that it should be easy to find such a counting number (360 is an obvious candidate), in fact, no such counting number exists.

53. $1 + 2 + 3 + 4 + 5 + 6 + 7 + (8 \times 9) = 100$. Other solutions are possible.

54. $123 - 45 - 67 + 89 = 100$ holds the record. Here are some of the other solutions that you may have obtained:

$$1 + 2 + 34 - 5 + 67 - 8 + 9 = 100$$
$$12 + 3 - 4 + 5 + 67 + 8 + 9 = 100$$
$$123 - 4 - 5 - 6 - 7 + 8 - 9 = 100$$
$$123 + 4 - 5 + 67 - 89 = 100$$
$$123 + 45 - 67 + 8 - 9 = 100$$

55. $98 - 76 + 54 + 3 + 21 = 100$. Other solutions are left for you to figure out.

56.   Yes.

It may be easier to begin with a simpler case. Mrs. Poorhouse only has a round cardtable that seats four, but she also uses placecards. When all her guests sit in the wrong place, instead of having a butler and maids march around the table, she rotates the table until one of the cards is in the proper place. The

question is whether or not she can rotate
the table until two of the cards are in
the proper place. It is easy to see that
she can always get the card in the proper
place for each person, although the remaining cards may be all wrong. Now
there are four different positions the
table can occupy in all, but one of them
is the original position in which everyone is wrongly placed. Therefore, there
are only three different positions to consider for the table. Call these positions A,
B, and C, and the original position I. No
one is seated correctly in position I. One
quarter turn brings position A. If no one
or only one person is seated correctly in
position A, then everyone (but possibly
one person) was at least two places away
from the correct position. Another quarter turn brings you to position B. If no
one or only one person is seated correctly at position B, then everyone (but
possibly two persons) was at least three
places away from the correct position.
The third quarter turn brings you to position C, which is the only other position
for the table. If one person is correct,
then someone else must have been four
places away from the correct position—
but that cannot be, since four places
away would be the correct position.
Since that cannot be, there must be one

of the positions, A, B, or C, when at least two persons are in the correct position.

The same argument applies to any number of places, including twenty-four. There are twenty-three positions of the table to consider, but there are twenty-four persons to be placed. At one of the twenty-three positions, there must be two people given their own card.

57.   5 kilometers. The rate at which the trains are traveling is $\frac{180}{60}$ or three kilometers per minute for the passenger train and $\frac{120}{60}$ or two kilometers per minute for the freight train. This means that their combined speed of approach is five kilometers per minute. Since they were warned one minute before the collision, they were five kilometers apart, enough time to stop and prevent the collision.

58.   The older sister gave the younger sister two one-dollar bills.

The first thing to note is that if each sheep sold for the same price in dollars as the number in the herd, then the total price is the square of the number in the herd. (If the herd was, say, three sheep, selling for $3 each, the total price would be $9.) The second is that there must be an odd number of $10 bills. If there had been an even number, and the older sister took the first, then the younger sister would get the last (and there would be no complaint). In fact, there must be at least three tens for the younger sister to have received even one ten-dollar bill.

Look at the squares that can be divided by 10 with a remainder. Which ones have an odd number of tens? Since 0 is an even number, the first square that contains an odd number of tens is 16. You have to eliminate 25 since it has an even number of tens. You can accept 36, but 64 and 81 have an even number of tens. Therefore, for any single-digit number, the square contains an odd number of tens only if the square ends in 6 (that is, 16 and 36 are the only ones with an odd number of tens). The total cost cannot be 100 dollars, since that is an even number of tens.

If the number being squared is greater than 10 but less than 100, then it is of the form $(10 + n)$, where n is some number. The square of $(10 + n)$ is $100 + 20n + n^2$, which will always have an even number of tens if the square of n has an even number of tens since $100 + 20n$ is an even number of tens. Therefore, for all the numbers less than 100 squared, if there is an odd number of tens, the square ends in the digit 6. In fact, this same argument can be extended to any size number. Thus, there

were six silver dollars no matter how
many ten-dollar bills were involved.

If the older sister had ten dollars more
than the younger sister before the silver
dollars were dispersed, then after the
younger sister got the silver dollars, the
older one had $4 more than the younger.
Therefore, to even the account, the older
sister gave the younger one two one-dollar bills.

59.   Here is the next-to-last step. The
dashed lines indicate the final square,
while the solid lines show the five
pieces. If you cut the triangles where
they are crossed by the dashed lines, the
pieces that are cut off can be used to fill
out the final square.

60.   The rule is that the Soma pieces
consist of all figures formed from fewer
than five cubes joined along their faces
that are not rectangular prisms. There are
at least 230 different ways to form a cube
from the seven Soma pieces. It is sug-
gested that a good strategy is to start
forming the three-by-three-by-three

cube with the pieces labeled E, F, and G, then fill in the spaces with the other pieces, saving A for last.

61. There are eight equilateral triangles in the figure. For the record, the triangles are CGD, MJN, BJE, LGO, BHD, LHN, CIE, and MIO. Another figure formed from six line segments that has eight equilateral triangles is the familiar Star of David.

62. The solution is completed as follows: You have assumed that the problem has been solved, which of course it has not been. If the canyon did not exist, the answer would be a straight line between Tran and Slate. Similarly, if Tran were on the edge of the canyon instead of some distance away, a bridge straight across the canyon and a road from the end of the bridge to Slate would be the answer. The secret is to combine all these ideas by forming a parallelogram that has the bridge as one side and whose adjacent side is the road from Tran to the bridge. The opposite side

of the parallelogram, however, is the one you find first. Start at Tran and mark off a distance toward the canyon, perpendicular to it and equal to the width of the canyon. This locates a point uniquely. You stand at that point. Now sight Slate from that point and have a volunteer move along the far wall of the canyon until the volunteer is in line with Slate. The line between where you stand and Slate is the shortest distance from you to Slate. Where the volunteer stands locates the end of the Slate side of the bridge. The Tran side of the bridge will be directly across from it.

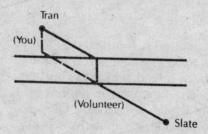

Roads can go straight from Tran and Slate to the bridge, giving the minimum possible cost for the Tran-Slate Way since the distance from Tran to the bridge is the same as the distance from your point to the Slate end of the bridge.

63. 314 square feet to the nearest foot.
Bob realized that since the Professor was
a mathematician, he must have had
some way to determine the area from
the single measurement of twenty feet.
Therefore, the area must be determined
by that measurement. Twenty feet is the
length of the line segment from one
edge of the larger circle to the other
edge when the line segment just touches
the smaller circle. Given that line segment, the area must be the same no
matter what the sizes of the two circles
are (or else the Professor was not a very
good mathematician). In particular, if the
smaller circle became very small, and the
length of the line segment stayed the
same, the size of the larger circle would
also become smaller. When the smaller
circle became a point, the line segment
would become the diameter of the larger
circle. Now a circle has an area that is pi
times the square of the radius, so if the
diameter is twenty feet, the radius is ten
feet, and the area is about 314 square
feet.

64. 4 yards (or 12 feet).
It helps to draw in the diagonals of the
rectangle and a cross along the middle
of the rectangle (see Illustration, p.
122).

$$a^2 + 3^2 = 5^2$$
$$a^2 = 25 - 9 \text{ or } 16$$
$$a = 4$$

Clearly, the length of half a diagonal of the rectangle is the same as the radius of the circle, or five yards. One of these half diagonals is equal to the length of the other diagonal of a small rectangle; for example, OC is equal to GF. Therefore, you know that OF is three yards and OC is five yards. This is a right triangle so you can use the Pythagorean theorem to find OE, which is the distance Jack dived.

65.   The bear is white, and the bird is black and white.

Both of these cheat a little, since the bear puzzle assumes that polar bears are found at the North Pole while the bird puzzle assumes that penguins are found at the South Pole. In each case, it is a little out of their normal range, but close enough for puzzle purposes.

The bear: From the North Pole, if a traveler goes a mile south, a mile east, and a mile north, it is clear that the traveler will once again wind up at the North Pole. If the traveler is a bear, it is most likely (by far) to be a polar bear, and, of course, white.

The bird: A bird that walks for three miles clearly cannot fly. Since there are no birds living near the North Pole that cannot fly, you have to look for someplace else on the globe that meets the conditions. The only other place that a traveler can make the journey described is from a place near the South Pole. Suppose, for example, that the bird begins the walk somewhere around 1.16 miles north of the South Pole. It walks one mile south. Then it turns and walks one mile east. Since the circumference of a circle with a radius of 0.16 miles is just a tiny fraction over a mile, essentially the bird walks around the South Pole, returning to the point where it first turned east. Then, if it walks north for a mile, it will be back where it started. Since the only bird in Antarctica that cannot fly is the penguin, the bird must be a penguin. Therefore, it is black and white.

66. Oddly enough, even if you eliminate the rule that the quilt must be cut along the edges of the squares, this is the only possible solution.

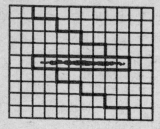 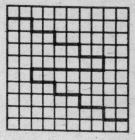

67.   96 blocks. Pi is four, and the taxicab circle is a set of isolated points in the shape of a square. Here, for the sake of the size of the drawing, is a taxicab circle that has a radius of four blocks. It is easy to verify that all the isolated points in the taxicab circle are exactly four blocks from the center of the taxicab circle. Notice that Max could either drive along the path that takes him alternatively five blocks from the center or that takes him three blocks from the center, but in each case, he would travel the same distance (he could also switch back and forth between these paths at random). In any case, his distance traveled would be thirty-two blocks around the taxicab circle. This is the circumference of the taxicab circle. Since the diameter of the taxicab circle is eight blocks, this makes pi equal to $\frac{32}{8}$, or 4.

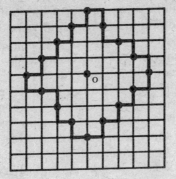

It is easy to see that the larger taxicab circle with a radius of twelve blocks would also be a set of isolated points in the shape of a square. The distance Max would travel around this circle is ninety-six blocks.

68. Loretta should move into the same building that Faye is going to live in. If Loretta's only friends were Alice and Kathleen, then she could live anywhere between their two buildings and the total distance to each of her friends would be the same. Clearly, if Loretta lived somewhere not between Alice and Kathleen, then the total distance would be greater than that. Similarly, if she lives anywhere between Bryan and Jack, the total distance will be the minimum for that pair also, so if you consider just Alice, Bryan, Jack, and Kathleen, the total

distance will be a minimum for the four friends if Loretta lives between Bryan and Jack. You can work your way in, pair by pair, through to Ed and George. At this point, considering just the ten friends so paired, Loretta can achieve her goal by living anywhere between Ed and George. Now consider how to minimize Loretta's distance from Faye. If Loretta moves into the same building, that distance will be zero, so moving into Faye's building is the solution to the problem.

69. Arrange the one-yen coins along the line in the pattern shown below. Then use your straightedge along the dashed lines to mark the desired length.

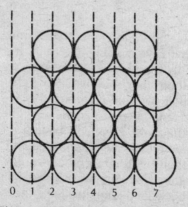

70. The sentence "This sentence is in English" when translated into another language, say French, should have the

same truth value as it does in English. No sentence should be permitted to change from true to false just because of the language in which it is expressed. The sentence "This sentence uses five words" would be accepted as a true sentence if it were not for the fact that it talks about itself. To write the negation of a sentence, the most general way is to say "it is not the case that" in front of the original sentence. However, "It is not the case that this sentence used five words" would also be accepted as true (if it did not talk about itself).

71. There can be no number that meets this description, since—by the rules set forth—you would have to accept the expression *the least number that cannot be named in a hundred letters and spaces or fewer* as a name for the number. But that expression contains only 78 letters and spaces, which is fewer than the hundred set forth in the description of the number's shortest name. Sometimes in mathematics you can describe something that does not exist, such as a triangle with four sides or the fraction with whole numbers as numerators and denominators whose square is two.

72. The unit to be used is ¼ the length of a side of the square. If you call this

unit a quadrimeter, then the side of the square is four quadrimeters long. Therefore, the perimeter is sixteen quadrimeters. The area is the square of four quadrimeters, or sixteen square quadrimeters. Therefore, the number of units in the perimeter is always equal to the number of units in the area—if you choose the right unit.

73.   To find a square with the same area as the circle, if the circle has the diameter d, then you need to find a square whose area is $\frac{1}{4}\pi d$, but the square erected on the diameter has an area of d^2. Only if π were equal to four would this method work.

74–77.   No answers.